Kingdom Living
Small Group Series

The Character of God

Understanding His Heart for Us

Kingdom Living
Small Group Series

The Character of God

UNDERSTANDING HIS
HEART FOR US

ampelōn
PUBLISHING

Kingdom Living — The Character of God: Understanding His Heart for Us
Copyright ©2007 by Brian T. Anderson & Glynnis Whitwer

Unless otherwise noted, scripture quotations taken from the HOLY BIBLE, NEW INTERNATIONAL VERSION. NIV. Copyright © 1973, 1978, 1984 by International Bible Society. Used by permission of Zondervan Publishing House. All rights reserved.

Scripture quotations marked (NASB) taken from the New American Standard Bible®, Copyright © 1960, 1962, 1963, 1968, 1971, 1972, 1973, 1975, 1977, 1995 by The Lockman Foundation. Used by permission.

Scripture quotations marked (LB) taken from The Living Bible, Copyright © by Kenneth N. Taylor, 1971. Used by permission of Tyndale House Publishers, Inc.

All rights reserved. No part of this publication may be reproduced in any form or by any means — electronic, mechanical, photocopy, recording, or any other — except for brief quotations in printed reviews, without the prior permission of the publisher.

ISBN: 978-0-9786394-3-3

Printed in the United States of America
First printing

Requests for information should be addressed to:
Ampelon Publishing
6920 Jimmy Carter Blvd., Suite 200
Norcross, GA 30071
To order other Ampelon Publishing products, visit us on the web at:
www.ampelonpublishing.com

Contents

How to use this study guide 7

Introduction to The Character of God 11

Lesson One:
God Is Sovereign.................. 13

Lesson Two:
God Never Changes 21

Lesson Three:
God's Amazing Grace 29

Lesson Four:
God Can Be Trusted 37

Lesson Five:
God Is Always Near.................. 45

Lesson Six:
God Loves You 51

Leader's Guide 59

THE KINGDOM LIVING BIBLE STUDY SERIES

The kingdom of God is not defined by mighty fortress walls, colorful pennants fluttering in the breeze, or mounted saints on powerful steeds. It's not a place where sentries patrol castle walls and moats deter intruders. The kingdom of God isn't a place we can visit, but it's as real as any empire known to man.

The kingdom of God is really a kingdom within a kingdom. It's a spiritual kingdom, ushered in by Jesus, where God reigns over everything. It is both a present reality and a future hope. And yet it exists in the midst of the kingdoms of this earth, where Satan rules.

The Israelites had been promised this kingdom of God, also referred to as the kingdom of heaven in the book of Matthew. They had been waiting thousands of years for the promised King who would restore them to power and save them from their suffering. So when John the Baptist proclaimed, "Repent, for the kingdom of heaven is near" (Matthew 3:2), they listened.

Jesus said those same words Himself in Matthew 4:17. In fact, the message of the kingdom of God was the reason Jesus said He came. When the people of Capernaum wanted Jesus to stay longer, He said, "I must preach the good news of the kingdom of God to the other towns also, because that is why I was sent" (Luke 4:43). Christianity did not start with the story of the resurrection of Jesus—that hadn't happened. People repented and turned to God through the teachings and the reality of the kingdom of heaven.

Jesus modeled the life of a subject of the kingdom of heaven. As He walked from city to city, He invested His life in others, taught, preached the good news of the kingdom, cared for the poor, healed the sick, and cast out demons. Jesus showed us that the kingdom of God is where God's Word is being taught and His work is being done.

As believers today, we are called to continue the works of Jesus and advance the kingdom of God. Jesus said, "Truly, truly, I say to you, he who believes in Me, the works that I do, he will do also; and greater works than these he will do; because I go to the Father" (John 14:12, NASB). However, as people of the Kingdom, we are also thrust into a war with God's enemies. How do we obey the commands of Jesus, yet battle an unseen enemy?

The key to walking in the power of the kingdom of God is learning to do what the Father is doing in each situation. Jesus Himself acknowledged His dependence on God: "Therefore Jesus answered and was saying to them, 'Truly, truly, I say to you, the Son can do nothing of Himself, unless it is something He sees the Father doing; for whatever the Father does, these things the Son also does in like manner'" (John 5:19, NASB).

In this Kingdom Living Bible Study Series, we will delve deeply into what living life as a follower of Jesus is all about. We'll study Scripture and apply the Word of God to our hearts and lives. We'll learn how to live like Christ, how to watch for what the Father is doing, experience transformation, and impact our community with the Good News of the Gospel.

Life in the kingdom of God is exciting! We invite you to pursue following Jesus with all your heart and get ready for an adventure. Kingdom living will transform your life.

Small Group Tips

These studies are designed for personal or group studies. If you are participating in a group, we would like to share some tips for making it a great experience.

First, congratulations on taking this step to develop community with other believers! We weren't meant to be isolated Christians. After Pentecost, there were 3,000 believers in Jerusalem. Acts 2:42 says, "They devoted themselves to the apostles' teaching and to the fellowship, to the breaking of bread and to prayer." Imagine 3,000 believers, passionate about their love for God, meeting in homes for fellowship, teaching and prayer. Oh, yes, ... and food!

Small groups were one of the first ways the kingdom of God was advanced. Acts 2:46-47 tells us more about these first believers: "Every day they continued to meet together in the temple courts. They broke bread in their homes and ate together with glad and sincere hearts, praising God and enjoying the favor of all the people. And the Lord added to their number daily those who were being saved." Meeting in large groups, meeting in homes in small groups, praising God and sharing the Good News—what an amazing picture of community.

As you embark on this study, we encourage you to open your heart to what God might want to do during your small group time. Here are some ideas on how to prepare:

1. Before each group meeting, do your best to be prepared—pray about and get familiar with the content of that week's Bible study.

2. Pray for your group beforehand. Pray for your leaders, the hosts, and the other people in the group.

3. Watch for God to speak to you during the small group. This could be during worship, prayer, through another member of the group, or quietly in your heart.

4. Be open to meeting with people different from you. God may specifically put you in a group so you can learn from others with different experiences and insights.

5. Be transparent. You don't have to spill your guts, but be willing to share your personal struggles when appropriate. This is how trust develops in a group.

6. Be yourself. God has called you into His service just how you are. You don't have to try and be like anybody else. Guard your heart against comparisons.

7. Protect confidentiality. What is shared in the group, stays in the group.

8. Look for one idea to apply to your life today. Allow God's Word to change your life one small step at a time.

BIBLE STUDY BASICS

Studying the Bible can seem overwhelming. It doesn't have to be. Our goal with this series is to learn more about life in the kingdom of God bit by bit. God wants us to understand His Word and will open our ears and hearts when we approach Bible study with a willing heart. Here are some tips to get you started:

1. Pray before doing your lesson. Ask God to teach you from the Scriptures and to speak to you through the Holy Spirit.

2. Read the Scripture reference several times. If it's a familiar verse, read it out loud to gain a new perspective. Read it in different versions if you have them. (www.biblegateway.com and www.crosswalk.com offer many versions on line)

3. If you have a Bible with study notes, read them. Read any cross-references (often indicated by a small letter after a word).

4. Read with expectancy that God will teach you from His Word. Don't try to make the Scripture say what you want it to say.

5. Look for the main theme of each passage, look for the context (read before and after the verse), and identify how the central truth applies to you.

6. Answer the questions to the best of your ability. If you are unsure of an answer, that's OK. Share that with the group and ask for their help in understanding the passage or question.

7. Thank God for the gift of the Bible and for teaching you through it.

We pray that God will touch you in a deep and intimate way as you study His Word and apply yourself to becoming a passionate follower of Jesus. May God bless you richly.

The Character of God

"I know Him ... and I know He loves me!" Her face shined with confident knowledge. Jody knew that in spite of the difficulties she was experiencing, God was working things out for her good. The peace of this truth settled her worried mind, and her outlook was one of optimism instead of despair.

Knowing God makes all the difference in how we deal with life. Not knowing about God, like we know about the life of a historical character by reading a biography. But really knowing God as we know a friend. We can know and understand His character, we can know His love and know His heart for us!

The Bible says that we can all get to know God personally. This is a process, just like getting to know anyone. Consider how you got to know your best friend. Your friendship likely started by sharing a common interest or need. As time went on, you shared your thoughts and feelings. Really good friends know how the other will respond in a given situation; they know the true character of each other. This takes time.

Today, we get to know God in a similar fashion. Over time, through experiencing God in daily life and by reading His words in the Bible, we come to know God. Just as we learn a lot about a person by watching how he or she acts, we know God by His actions and deeds recorded in Scripture. The Bible tells us Moses spoke these words to God, "If you are pleased with me, *teach me your ways* so I may know you and continue to find favor with you" (Exodus 33:13, *emphasis ours*). God's ways reveal who God really is.

God also chose to reveal Himself to us by coming to earth as a man—Jesus Christ. The Apostle John wrote this about Jesus, "No one has ever seen God, but God the One and Only, who is at the Father's side, has made him known" (John 1:18).

Although knowing God is possible, it's not always easy to understand God's ways. Isaiah 55:8 tells us, "'For my thoughts are not your thoughts, neither are your ways my ways,' declares the Lord." God's ways are different than man's ways. Sometimes it's hard to comprehend the attributes of God. We wonder how God can love someone who hates Him? How can God forgive the most heinous sin? How can God care about the details of our lives? As we get to know God, we learn that all God's attributes culminate in love.

God knows that as we get to know Him, we will grow in our trust and love as well. Then, the more we love Him, the more we want to know Him. It's a great cycle!

In this study, we look at six attributes of God's character that help us know Him more and understand His heart for us. We'll learn of His ever-nearness, consistency, grace, sovereignty, faithfulness and love. God openly reveals Himself to us, and this study explores some truths about God's character found in the Bible.

Jeremiah 29:13 offers these words of hope from God: "You will seek me and find me when you seek me with all your heart."

One

[GOD IS SOVEREIGN]

But our God is in the heavens; He does whatever He pleases.
Psalm 115:3 (NASB)

The Bible teaches that God is Sovereign. Simply put, that means He's in control of everything. Why? Because He created everything. Take nature for example. Not only did God create nature, but He also sustains it. When He wants to overrule nature and perform a miracle, then He overrules it! It's His prerogative!

King David acknowledged God's sovereignty in 1 Chronicles 29:11: "Yours, O Lord, is the greatness, the power, the glory, the victory, and the majesty. Everything in the heavens and on earth is yours, O Lord, and this is your kingdom. We adore you as the one who is over all things" (NLT).

God is also in control of history. The Bible teaches that everything is moving towards a climax. There's a plan and a purpose for everything in our past, present and future. History is moving towards a climax, and God's in control of that.

Not only is God in control of nature and history, but He's also in control of our lives. None of us chose our birth date or birthplace. Nor did we choose our parents. We didn't get to decide our natural talents or abilities. God chose all of those details, and He did so for a purpose … His purpose.

Although we have lots of freedom to choose how we act, we don't choose the consequences of our actions. God has preordained those as well.

On the surface it would seem we live a restrictive life. One might wonder the point in planning anything if God's already decided the outcome. However, although God reserves the right to call the shots, it's not as a dictator. That's why He gave us free will. Because God created and sustains everything, He also holds the key to an abundant, joy-filled life. God's way is really the best way.

The world tells us to make our own path, to do it "my way." The world teaches us to live like it's "my way or the highway." Yet the Bible teaches that true freedom comes from living under the loving care of our Heavenly Father. Understanding how God's sovereignty impacts our lives helps us enjoy a life of greater meaning and purpose. In this study we'll look at three ways God's sovereignty affects us: We understand that our plans are limited, our problems have a purpose and our prayers make a difference.

<<< Let'sTalk

1) Identify some pre-ordained consequences to our actions or behaviors. (One example would be a ticket for speeding.)

2) What natural abilities or talents do you have? (These are abilities that you have had from an early age.)

<<< EnteringIn
[My plans are limited.]

Read Proverbs 19:21.

3) Based on Proverbs 19:21, what needs to happen for our plans to "succeed"?

4) Have you ever planned to do something, but then circumstances changed your plans? Describe that situation.

[BytheWay]
[If God is sovereign, why doesn't He stop all evil plans? This is the question of the ages. Living in this tension between God's sovereignty and our free will is part of living in the Kingdom of God. Remember, the Kingdom of God is both here and not here at the same time! Although God is Sovereign, it does not mean He controls all events. He knows what events will take place, but that doesn't mean He makes them happen or controls them totally.]

5) It's easy to assume an attitude that says, "I don't need God and can figure life out on my own." What are some of the dangers of this type of thinking?

6) What are some benefits of submitting our will to God's will?

[My problems have a purpose.]

Read 1 Peter 1:6-7.

7) According to this passage, what is one of the positive results of the trials we experience? How does this benefit Christians?

8) Have you ever seen good come out of a bad situation? Describe.

[BytheWay]

[Romans 8:28 says, "And we know that God causes all things to work together for good to those who love God, to those who are called according to His purpose." This Scripture brings hope and comfort when we are overwhelmed with problems. Note that this promise is given for those who love God and who are called to His purpose.]

9) How does knowing that God uses trials for your good help you deal with life's problems?

10) What are some ways we can focus more on God's power over our circumstances?

[My prayers make a difference.]

Read Matthew 7:7-11.

11) What is Jesus telling us about God's character and abilities in Matthew 7:7-11?

12) Since God already knows what we need, why would He want His children to ask for His help?

13) What are some reasons God doesn't answer every one of our prayers exactly as we pray them?

<<< **PuttingFeettoit**

14) How can you include God in your planning and goal setting?

15) What situations or relationships in your life seem to be beyond your control this week? Realize that they are not out of God's control and seek God's help in prayer.

<<< TakingitwithYou

Romans 8:28: "And we know that God causes all things to work together for good to those who love God, to those who are called according to His purpose" (NASB).

<<< Journal

Two

[GOD NEVER CHANGES]

Whatever is good and perfect comes to us from God above, who created all heaven's lights. Unlike them, he never changes or casts shifting shadows.

James 1:17 (NLT)

Most of us have a love-hate relationship with change. We love the convenience technology brings to our lives–such as e-mail and text messaging–and yet we miss the days when people actually spoke in complete sentences instead of sound bytes. We love the idea of a digital camera and video, but then can't figure out how to actually print or store our pictures and videos. Exterior change–that which happens to us–brings with it an uncertainty, and quite often frustration.

While a lot of change is good, like getting a raise or becoming physically fit, that's not the change that troubles us. It's the negative change that drags us down. In fact, every list of the top stress-causing events in life involves some type of change. Everyday change and significant life-altering change cause stress. Too much change in too short a time period can crush even the strongest individual.

In addition to the change happening around us, we are constantly changing. If you haven't noticed, take a look in the mirror. Bob Dylan sang a song with these lyrics: "The times, they are a-changin'" We could say something similar today, "The lines they are a-changin'" … the hairline, the waist line and the credit line!

In a world where change is the norm, is anything permanent? Is there anything that is reliable and never changes? The answer is "yes!" God never changes!

Malachi 3:6a says, "For I, the Lord, do not change." God is always the same. He has always been, and He always will be! In a stress-filled world where everything changes, we can stabilize our lives by focusing on three ways God never changes: God's love for us never changes, God's Word never changes, and God's purpose for our lives never changes. God's consistency brings peace and confidence in our ever-changing world.

<<< Let's Talk

1) Identify one change in your life—something within the last year—that has brought some frustration with it.

2) If you could change one thing about yourself personally, what would it be?

<<< EnteringIn
[God's love for me never changes.]

Read Jeremiah 31:3-4.

[BytheWay]
[Jeremiah speaks God's words of "everlasting love" in spite of the wrong done by the Israelites. Some of these offenses included sacrificing their own children to other gods, worshiping idols and abandoning their covenant with God. Although there were consequences to be paid, God's love for His people never failed.]

3) Has someone ever loved you in spite of something you have done wrong? Describe some of the characteristics of that person. How did his or her love make you feel?

4) The Israelites had been unfaithful to God. In fact, Jeremiah refers to them as an unfaithful wife (3:20). In spite of that, how does God address them? What does this term tell you about God's faithful love?

5) The Israelites suffered greatly because of their unfaithfulness. Yet, God promises to build them up again. How does God's love build you up and draw you to Him?

[God's Word never changes.]

Read Isaiah 40:8.

6) List some laws in our nation's history, or your local community/state that have changed over time. Have those changes been good or bad?

7) What are some biblical commandments, either from the Old Testament or the commands of Jesus, that people dismiss as out-of-date or impractical?

8) At the time Isaiah spoke the words of prophecy found in Isaiah 40, the Israelites had been in Babylonian captivity for years. Imagine being in a foreign land, far from everything you knew and loved. What would the constancy of God's Word mean to you?

[BytheWay]
[The Bible is the number one best-selling book of all time. It was written by 40 men over a period of about 1600 years dating from 1500 BC to about 100 years after Christ. These men wrote this Scripture as God inspired them. Second Timothy 3:16 tells us this about the Bible: "All Scripture is God-breathed and is useful for teaching, rebuking, correcting and training in righteousness ..."]

9) How should knowing that God's Word will never change alter your approach to reading the Bible?

10) What will happen if you make life-decisions based on something that changes all the time, like your feelings, or other people's opinions? What will happen if you base your life on God's unchanging Word?

[God's purpose for my life will never change.]

Read Psalm 33:11.

11) What does Psalm 33:11 tell us about God's plans?

12) What are some reasons our plans change?

13) What are some of God's plans for our lives? To get some ideas, read Jeremiah 29:11, John 10:10 and Romans 8:29.

14) Does God's purpose for your life always get fulfilled? Why or why not?

[BytheWay]

[God's greatest purpose for each of us is that we would receive His Son, Jesus Christ, as our Savior and Lord. In other words, God wants us to be saved from eternal separation from Him. Romans 10:9 says, "That if you confess with your mouth Jesus as Lord, and believe in your heart that God raised Him from the dead, you will be saved" (NASB).]

<<< PuttingFeettoit

15) What are the personal benefits to you of believing that God's love, His Word and His purposes never change?

16) Although God never changes, people often need to change. What are some ways you need to change to be more obedient to God's Word and His purpose for your life?

<<< TakingitwithYou

Psalm 33:11: "The counsel of the LORD stands forever, the plans of His heart from generation to generation" (NASB).

<<< Journal

Three

[GOD'S AMAZING GRACE]

But you, O LORD, are a compassionate and gracious God, slow to anger, abounding in love and faithfulness.

Psalm 86:15a

Most of us can easily fill in the blanks in the following statements:
- There's no such thing as a free _____!
- If it sounds too good to be true, it probably _____.
- God helps those who help _____.

Chances are you've probably even said something similar before. Why? Most of us follow the philosophy that says, "You get what you pay for, and you get what you deserve!" This is admirable in one sense because it means there's an inherent preference for fairness in the world. If I work hard, I'll earn money. On the other hand, if I come in late and leave early, I'll probably get fired. That's just fair! Our innate longing for justice surfaces when someone else gets what we think they "deserve," especially when it's not pleasant.

We live in a world full of people trying to earn the approval of others, or work hard enough to get ahead. Into this world of striving, entered Jesus with a new message: God doesn't think like we do! In spite of what people thought, they couldn't "earn" God's favor, or work hard enough to get into heaven. No matter how hard they tried, they couldn't make God love them. This is difficult to understand when all your life you've worked hard to get where you are today.

Jesus introduced the concept of "Grace." The psalmist had spoken about God's gracious nature. But now grace took on an entirely new meaning. Grace, meaning God's undeserved good will, loving-kindness and favor, was offered personally to each of them ...

and to each of us. This means we don't have to earn God's love and generosity—He offers it freely.

God operates on the "law" of grace. Instead of giving us what we deserve, He gives us what we need. He is a merciful Heavenly Father, who is pleased to shower blessings on His beloved children. God's grace makes a profound difference in our lives. In this study we will look at three ways God's grace changes us: it removes our guilt, it strengthens our resolve, and it keeps us going when life is difficult.

<<< Let'sTalk

1) What is one of the best gifts you've ever received?

2) Have you ever gotten off the hook when you've done something wrong? Describe.

<<< EnteringIn
[God's saving grace removes my guilt.]

Read Ephesians 2:8-9.

[BytheWay]
[The word "saved" in Ephesians 2:8 is the Greek word *sozo* meaning "to preserve one who is in danger of destruction." Many Christians describe themselves as "saved." They use this term to describe what faith in Jesus Christ has done for them, such as saving them from a life of despair and from a life eternally separated from God.]

Three: God's Amazing Grace

3) Based on this verse, how do we receive salvation?

4) Although we are saved "through faith," even this doesn't come from us. How is faith a "gift of God"? What are our responsibilities regarding faith?

5) What are some ways people try to "earn" their salvation?

6) We are all guilty because we have all sinned (Romans 3:22-23). But God doesn't want us to feel guilty. How does the truth of this Scripture wash away our guilt?

[God's strengthening grace helps me stand firm.]

Read Hebrews 13:9.

7) The "heart" of a person was considered the whole of his or her inner life–his or her thoughts and emotions. What is a Christian's best source of strength, according to this verse, and how does it strengthen our hearts?

8) The early Christians had to balance the Old Testament dietary laws with their new freedom in Christ. Some still tried to find strength and approval by following the "rules." How does following "rules" today, whether in church or other areas of life, give us a false sense of strength and security?

9) The "strange teachings" referred to in this verse meant anything foreign to the Gospel of Jesus Christ. How can understanding God's grace help us stand firm against wrong teaching?

Three: God's Amazing Grace

[God's sustaining grace keeps me going when the going gets tough.]

Read II Corinthians 12:7-10.

[BytheWay]
[When we pray about a problem, one of two things is going to happen: 1) God may remove the problem, or 2) God will supply sustaining grace for us to handle the problem. Either way, we can trust God to take care of us and our needs.]

10) Paul, the writer of Second Corinthians, makes it clear that the "thorn" in his flesh was given for a spiritual benefit. What is that benefit according to this passage? Why might Paul consider that a benefit?

11) What are some other reasons God might allow us to experience problems?

12) How is Jesus' power made perfect in our weakness?

13) What happens if we don't depend on God's grace when faced with a problem?

<<< PuttingFeettoit

Read James 4:6b.

14) What is the key to receiving God's grace in your life? Describe why pride keeps us from receiving God's grace.

15) What are some specific ways you can choose humility in your everyday life?

<<< TakingitwithYou

Ephesians 2:8-9: "For by grace you have been saved through faith; and that not of yourselves, it is the gift of God; not as a result of works, so that no one may boast." (NASB).

<<< Journal

Four

[GOD CAN BE TRUSTED]

For no matter how many promises God has made, they are "Yes" in Christ. And so through him the "Amen" is spoken by us to the glory of God.

2 Corinthians 1:20

It's easy to believe that God is faithful until something really horrible happens in your life. It could be a job loss, financial problems or illness. But when God doesn't remove the problem in a "reasonable" time period, our thoughts can quickly turn to questions about God's faithfulness: "Doesn't God see this mess I'm in?" "Doesn't He care?" "If God really loved me, He'd do something about this!"

Times of trouble test our faith. Do we really trust God? Or, do we just say we do? Will God really do what He promised to do?

We all know how devastating a broken promise can be. Someone promised to be faithful to you–but he wasn't. Someone promises to pay you back–but she doesn't. Someone promised to stop a sinful habit–but it continues. Unfortunately, instead of being an unbreakable covenant from one person to another, a promise is more like a temporary commitment, until something easier or more attractive comes along–or until our will power eases and selfish desire assumes control.

We've all been unfaithful in one way or another. There's only One whose Word is faultless, whose character is faithful and who keeps every promise He's ever made, and that's God. Today God still keeps His promises to us. While those around us may disappoint, God never does. God can be trusted!

In difficult times, it's easy to doubt that God can be trusted. We may think God has forgotten about us or that His promises apply only to "good" Christians. But the truth about God is that His promises stand firm for those who love Him. God's promises aren't based on His or our emotional status at any given moment.

In this study, we'll look at four ways God can be trusted. We'll learn we can trust God to give us guidance, defend us, reward our generosity and forgive our sins. God can be trusted in every area of life! This study is just a glimpse of God's faithfulness!

<<< Let'sTalk

1) Has anyone ever kept a promise to you even though it was hard for him or her to do so? Describe what happened, and how you felt.

2) What does it tell you about a person's character when he or she habitually breaks promises?

Four: God Can Be Trusted

<<< EnteringIn
[I can depend on God to give me guidance.]

Read Proverbs 3:5-6.

3) Name some sources people turn to for guidance in the world today.

4) How can our own understanding of people and situations lead us astray at times?

5) What are some ways we can acknowledge the Lord in our everyday lives?

6) The Bible is one of the major ways God gives us guidance. List some of the decisions you have made in the past year that have been based on a biblical truth.

[I can depend on God to settle the score.]

Read Romans 12:19.

[BytheWay]
[Jesus introduced a radical new way of dealing with enemies. Instead of plotting revenge when offended, we are to love! In Matthew chapter 5:43-44, Jesus said this: "You have heard that it was said, 'Love your neighbor and hate your enemy.' But I tell you: Love your enemies and pray for those who persecute you, that you may be sons of your Father in heaven." How we treat our enemies really matters to God.]

7) Most people in a civilized society don't actively seek revenge against others. However, there are small, often underhanded, ways we seek to "pay others back" for the wrong they've done us. What are some common ways we take "revenge" on others?

8) Why would God want us to not seek our own revenge?

9) Not only are we to NOT take revenge, but we are to forgive and love our enemies. What are some ways you've learned to love those who have hurt you?

Four: God Can Be Trusted

[I can depend on God to reward my generosity.]

Read Luke 6:38.

[BytheWay]
[The Greek word for "give" in Luke 6:38 is "Didomi." It simply means to give something to someone. Every day we are faced with opportunities to give to others. We give of our attention, our love, our finances, and our skills, to name a few. Christians are called to be generous in the way we give–no matter what it is.]

10) Luke 6:38 offers a beautiful promise to believers–that they will be given good things in overflowing proportions. However, there's a condition attached to this promise. What is that condition, and why do you think it's so important to God?

11) When you have been generous, what types of "rewards" have you received?

[I can depend on God to forgive my sins.]

Read 1 John 1:8-9.

[BytheWay]
[Recognizing and confessing our sins are important spiritual growth components. When we deny we have sinned, it's easy to deny responsibility for our actions. God calls us to an alertness about sin in order to confess it quickly, and with God's power, to avoid it in the future.]

12) Almost every promise in the Bible contains a condition. The passage we just studied in Luke 6 is one example. What is the condition found in 1 John 1:9 that must be met in order for God to forgive our sins?

13) When we don't confess our sin, 1 John 1:8 says "the truth is not in us." How does denying sin blind us to truth? Give some examples.

14) When we confess our sin, God's forgiveness of us is complete. The verb for "forgive" has at its root the idea of canceling a debt. How does God's forgiveness affect your everyday life?

<<< PuttingFeettoit

15) What characteristic of God's faithfulness means the most to you right now? Why?

16) Not only does God want us to trust Him, but He wants us to be faithful as well. What is an area of your life in which you need to be more faithful or trustworthy?

<<< TakingitwithYou

Proverbs 3:5-6: Trust in the LORD with all your heart and do not lean on your own understanding. In all your ways acknowledge Him, and He will make your paths straight" (NASB).

<<< **Journal**

Five

[GOD IS ALWAYS NEAR]

"If I go up to the heavens, you are there; if I make my bed in the depths, you are there. If I rise on the wings of the dawn, if I settle on the far side of the sea, even there your hand will guide me, your right hand will hold me fast."
Psalm 139:8-10

Have you ever wondered how God can hear every prayer request from the tiniest child in Africa to the mightiest mogul in America? At the same time! Our human minds can't comprehend this ability to hear, much less, answer the millions of prayers God must receive every day.

Not only does God hear everyone's prayers, He is also near to us. How can God be in Peru and Pennsylvania, Toronto and Tucson, and yet by your side right now? There is no place in the universe where God is not! Theologians call this attribute of God "omnipresence." God never has to go anywhere because He's already there! Jeremiah 23:24 says, "'Can anyone hide from me? Am I not everywhere in all the heavens and the earth?' asks the Lord" (NLT).

God is everywhere! He is not limited by space or time. He's not limited to a single location. That's a hard concept for us to grasp because we are finite beings, with finite minds, living in a finite body. We often wish we could be in two places at once, but we can't. But it's no problem for God.

If we could grasp the reality of God's presence being everywhere, it would enrich our lives immensely. Imagine never feeling lonely, having God encourage you when you are tempted, feeling His confidence when you are worried and His loving arms of comfort when you are discouraged. In this lesson, we'll examine how God's presence changes and benefits our lives.

<<< Let's Talk

1) List some ways in which a close friend has enriched your life.

2) Think of a time you were lonely. What helped you through that time?

<<< Entering In
[When I'm lonely, God is my companion.]

Read Hebrews 13:5.

3) What are some of the reasons people feel lonely?

Five: God Is Always Near   47

4) What is the promise from God in Hebrews 13:5?

5) This promise comes immediately after a warning. What is the warning?

6) How can the love of money and being discontent lead to loneliness?

[When I'm tempted, God provides a way out.]

Read 1 Corinthians 10:13.

7) What does this verse say about temptation? What are some common temptations?

[BytheWay]
[James 1:13-14 tells us that God does not tempt us. "When tempted, no one should say, 'God is tempting me.' For God cannot be tempted by evil, nor does he tempt anyone ..." God does however test us at times. Satan tempts to get us to sin. God tests so that we are strengthened NOT to sin.]

8) How does God help us when we are tempted?

9) How does knowing God is present with you at every moment help you avoid temptation?

[When I'm worried, God is my confidence.]

Read Isaiah 43:2.

10) What does this verse say will happen when we go through trouble?

11) How should God's presence bring you confidence in difficult times?

[BytheWay]
[The book of Daniel, chapter three, tells the story of three men who went through actual fire because they wouldn't worship the gods of King Nebuchadnezzar. As punishment, Shadrach, Meshach and Abednego were tied up and thrown into a blazing furnace–yet survived! The Bible says that God walked through the fire with them! When they came out, their robes weren't scorched, and they didn't even smell like smoke!]

[When I'm discouraged, God is my comfort.]

Read Psalm 34:18.

12) What are the top sources of discouragement in your life?

13) List some of God's attributes which bring you comfort when you are discouraged.

<<< Putting Feet to it

14) One of the first steps to walking in the presence of God is to surrender every area of your life over to Jesus Christ. Identify any areas you are still holding control of.

15) One reason people don't feel God's presence is because they are just too busy and distracted. Name one activity you can give up this week in order to focus on the presence of God.

<<< Taking it with You

Psalm 145:17-18: "The LORD is righteous in all His ways and kind in all His deeds. The LORD is near to all who call upon Him, to all who call upon Him in truth." (NASB)

Six

[GOD LOVES YOU]

And may you have the power to understand, as all God's people should, how wide, how long, how high, and how deep his love really is.

Ephesians 3:18 (NLT)

What is love? Is it an emotion? Is it a verb? If you asked people on the street to define love, they'd probably call it a feeling. Is it the overwhelming feeling a parent gets looking in the face of his or her baby? Is it the butterflies-in-the-stomach feeling you get in a serious relationship? Is it how you feel looking at an all-you-can-eat pizza buffet? What is love?

The Bible has a definition for love, and it's not a feeling, emotion or verb. The Bible says that "God is love."

"Beloved, let us love one another, for love is from God; and everyone who loves is born of God and knows God. The one who does not love does not know God, for God is love" (1 John 4:7-8, NASB).

According to Scripture, love is defined by the character and actions of God! God's nature is loving, and His every action is loving. Consequently, we show that we know God when we love one another because that's who God is.

Unfortunately, many people haven't grasped the depth of God's love for them. They believe God's love is like the love other people have shown them. What a dangerous comparison! Human love can be fickle, unpredictable and even vengeful. People, especially those struggling with their own hurts and emotional damage, can warp the meaning of love, causing us to struggle with accepting God's love.

However, even love from the finest, most loving human being is only a shadow of God's rich love. Can we fully experience God's love? Can our human minds even begin to understand it? In Ephesians 3:18, the apostle Paul attempts to measure the immeasurable by conveying the breadth of God's love in human terms. It's wide, long, high and deep enough to reach everyone and everywhere! Paul knows it will take a supernatural power to understand God's love. As you begin this study, ask God in prayer for His power to understand His great love.

<<< Let's Talk

1) If you learned about love from watching television or movies, how would you describe it?

2) What is one thing someone could do or say that would prove he or she loved you?

Six: God Loves You

<<< EnteringIn

[BytheWay]
[Psalm 145:17 says, "The Lord is righteous in all his ways and loving toward all he has made" (NASB). This means that God's love is universal—He loves everyone in the world. The good new is that God loves me! The even better news is that God loves my enemies just as much as me! Why is that great news? Because someday, I might be someone's "enemy."]

[God's love is wide enough to include everybody.]

Read John 3:16-17.

3) According to these verses, what is the proof that God loves everyone?

4) John 3:16 tells us that God demonstrates His love by giving. What are some things (other than Jesus) that God offers to every human being that show His love?

5) Although God offers us the fullness of His love through our acceptance of Jesus, many people choose not to believe in Jesus. What are some reasons people refuse God's love?

6) First John 4:8 tells us that "God is love." However, when we read John 3:16 we learn that those who don't choose to believe in Jesus will "perish." What does this tell us about God's love?

[God's love is long enough to last forever.]

Read Psalm 89:2.

7) Name some types of human love that wear out after a short period of time.

Six: God Loves You 55

8) What are some reasons that human love changes over time or ceases to exist?

9) List some words that describe God's love.

[God's love is high enough to be everywhere.]

Read Romans 8:38-39.

10) Paul is eloquent and adamant in Romans 8:38-39 that nothing can come between God's love and us. Using these verses as a guide, give some examples of what can try and separate us from God's love, or convince us that God has stopped loving us.

11) Many people have trouble accepting that God loves them or experiencing His love for them. What can happen in the life of a Christian who doesn't know and experience God's love personally?

[BytheWay]
[God's love is deep enough to rescue us from the deepest, darkest places of sin. When you think you can go no lower, God is waiting with arms ready to catch you. Deuteronomy 33:27a says, "The eternal God is your refuge, and his everlasting arms are under you" (NLT). What a great safety net!]

[God's love is deep enough to meet my needs.]

Read Psalm 40:11.

12) Not only did God demonstrate His love by sending Jesus, but He continues to prove His love with His daily care. How has God met one or more of your needs this week?

13) It's easy for us to confuse our "wants" with our "needs." God, however, demonstrates His unfailing love by meeting our needs, not always our wants. How does this show God's love?

<<< PuttingFeettoit

14) Have you ever doubted God's love for you? What was the situation?

15) In light of God's great love for us, what should our response be? Is God prompting you to change anything in your life in light of His love?

<<< TakingitwithYou

Ephesians 3:18, "And may you have the power to understand, as all God's people should, how wide, how long, how high, and how deep his love is" (NLT).

<<< Journal

leader's guide

one

[GOD IS SOVEREIGN]

Question One

Life is filled with consequences. God designs some; others are found in our laws; and there are many determined by other people, such as teachers, parents, friends or a spouse.

We suffer from negative consequences when we choose the wrong path. Our bodies have some built-in consequences for misuse. If we drink too much alcohol, we'll get a hangover. If we listen to music too loud, we'll experience hearing loss. A thief goes to prison, a child is grounded for disobeying, and relationships are broken when trust is betrayed.

For the most part, we enjoy positive consequence when we follow the rules at school, keep the trust of a friend and make healthy choices about what we eat and drink.

Understanding natural consequences is a part of understanding God's Sovereignty. God says if you do certain things, then certain things are going to be the result. (Read Galatians 6:7-8)

Question Two

This question may be difficult for some to answer. After we've lived life awhile, we might think that some of our individual abilities and talents are there because we've developed them. That is certainly the truth! God gives each of us a measure of ability–what we do with it is up to us.

To answer this question, we must consider those talents and abilities we have a natural tendency toward. Students might identify those classes that seem to come "naturally." An athlete is gifted with certain physical talents. A scholar has mental abilities. Our sovereign God endowed each of us with specific talents for His purpose. It's up to us to identify those abilities as coming from God. Then, we can offer them back for His use.

Question Three

According to Proverbs 19:21, the success of our plans ultimately depends on the will of God. Those plans that conform to the purpose of God will ultimately prevail.

So how do we integrate this truth with the reality of the world? History books are filled with stories of atrocities committed against people. We see it every day on the news. Those plans certainly weren't in alignment with God's purposes!

This is a conflict that has existed since the beginning of time. We know there are things that happen in life that are not God's will. Sin is never God's will! God would never cause sin to happen. But sin happens because we live in a fallen world, with sinful people and an enemy who "prowls like a lion" looking to "steal, kill, and destroy" (John 10:10).

So what is our hope as Christians? Our hope is found in the truth of God's Word. We can be confident that God's plans will ultimately prevail and nothing can stand against them. Perhaps we need to start looking at life in terms of eternity. God's definition of successful plans isn't the same as ours.

Question Four

Most Christians have experienced God's re-direction in life. When we confess that Jesus is Lord of our life, we are saying that He is in charge. Once we state our allegiance to Jesus, then we are inviting Him to take control. This is particularly true for the Christian who regularly asks for God's help with decisions.

How many people thought they would marry the first great love of their life, only to marry someone different? Or how many people start one career, only to change direction? I (Brian) always wanted to be a professional baseball player. I played baseball all through school and went to college on a baseball scholarship. My senior year in college I had a transforming conversion to Christ, and all of my goals and dreams changed. Suddenly, all I wanted to do was serve God the best way I could.

I became a high school teacher and baseball coach. I thought I would do that the rest of my life. A few years into this, my wife and I started a Bible study in our home. It evolved into Vineyard

Church North Phoenix, and eventually I came to a place where I had to decide if God was calling me to pastor this church full time or keep teaching (we had about 200 people attending our church by this time--so continuing to do both wasn't an option any longer). My wife and I both felt God was directing me to pastor full time. So, I quit my job teaching and became a full time pastor.

God changed the entire direction of my life in a sovereign way, but He did it a little at a time. Often we can't "see" God directing our lives sovereignly until after the fact. At least that's how it happens with me most of the time.

Question Five

When we think we can figure out life on our own, that's presumption. Or, if we avoid asking God what He wants us to do with our lives, and follow our own way, that's presumption.

James offers a direct warning about making our own plans without direction from God. (Read James 4:13-16) This passage puts our plans into perspective. When we only consider what we want, we can become very self-centered. James calls making plans without considering God's will as evil boasting.

Question Six

Some people are so rigid in their planning, that if anything veers from their original plan, they get an ulcer. Stress, headaches, physical ailments, discontent and conflict are all consequences of a rigid life that denies God's sovereignty.

The flip side to a life of frustration is the peace that comes from trusting that God's plans are for our welfare. Not only does God have a good plan for our lives, but He also has the power to make it happen. Quite simply, it's a relief that we don't have to know it all! We just have to know the One who does! As long as we wrestle God for control, we will experience stress.

Trusting God is hard for many people, especially those who have been betrayed or hurt by someone in authority over them. Hurt people are suspicious and withhold trust, and it takes time to trust again. No one should be frustrated or angry by his or her inability to trust God. The Bible shows us that God welcomes our honesty. God knows the condition of our hearts and the depth of our pain. The best place to start is being honest with God and ourselves, and then asking God for help to trust again.

Question Seven

One thing that Peter says in 1 Peter 1:6-7 is that life is not a series of random events with no meaning. For followers of Christ, everything that enters our lives is filtered through God. That does not mean everything that happens is God's will; it does mean that God allows problems. Then He uses them for a greater purpose.

This passage teaches that some problems, or trials, are actually a necessary part of life. Obviously, this isn't referring to sinful problems, but those that are common to all of us. One benefit of trials is that our faith is tested in order to make it strong and pure. God in His sovereignty actually allows problems to make us stronger.

As Christians, we should be seeking to be more like Jesus every day. With that goal in mind, we can use every situation in life to assess our progress, especially trials. Jesus modeled suffering with love and kindness. We can use our own trials as a training ground for strengthening our faith.

Question Eight

Sometimes it takes years to find the good in a bad situation. Plus, we may need to see with eyes focused on eternity instead of this life. Romans 8:28 (found in the "By the Way" section) promises that God will cause all things to work for good to those who love Him. However, we may need to redefine "good." Knowing that God cares infinitely more about our character and our faith in Him, what seems good to us (keeping a job or good health) may actually not be good for us spiritually.

Question Nine

Hope is a crucial ingredient for an abundant life. In fact, trials can actually help produce hope in our lives according to Romans 5:3-5: "Not only so, but we also rejoice in our sufferings, because we know that suffering produces perseverance; perseverance, character; and character, hope. And hope does not disappoint us, because God has poured out his love into our hearts by the Holy Spirit, whom he has given us."

Hope isn't crossing our fingers and wishing that something good will happen out of our bad. For the Christian, hope is being sure that God will use trials for our good. It is having our hearts settled on that fact! When we have hope, then fear and uncertainty are removed in the midst of our problems. In fact, hope can even produce thankfulness because we know God is already at work.

Question Ten

We can start by not blaming God for our circumstances. Then we can look past the pain and difficulties and try to find God's purposes. Instead of being a victim of circumstances, we become an active participant in living out God's greater purpose for our lives and the lives of those around us.

One powerful way to focus more on God's power is through worship. When we lift God up through prayer or song, we become increasingly aware of His greatness. In worship, we get a different perspective on life when we turn our attention away from our problems and towards the One who can solve them. We get a God-perspective. With that perspective, we are assured of God's love and confident that God will act on our behalf. This brings great peace and comfort in the midst of a very uncertain world.

Question Eleven

Jesus is telling us that God has the character of a loving father, who only wants the best for His children. God is also a father who delights in giving good gifts to His children. Not only is God loving and generous, but He has the power to fulfill every request. As we've already learned, God doesn't always fulfill our requests, but He has the power to do so.

Question Twelve

Not only is God sovereign, but He's also omniscient, which means He already knows everything. So if God knows everything we need, why should we ask? One reason God wants us to ask for help is that it reminds us of our need for Him. Additionally, when we ask and then receive, we appreciate His work in our lives in greater measure. Asking God for help, and then watching Him answer, helps us know and love God more.

Question Thirteen

One reason God can't answer every prayer is that oftentimes there are competing prayers. Christians will sometimes pray in conflict with each other. One person prays for rain and another prays that it will be sunny. Christians pray for opposing sports teams. There's conflict between those prayers. Obviously, God can't answer both of them "yes."

Also, if God answered every one of our prayers, prayer would become a weapon of destruction. Imagine if God answered every angry employee's prayer about his or her boss! All bosses would be dead! While God is our defender, He is not a genie, ready to make our every wish His command. Plus, He's not going to answer any prayer that goes against His will.

Question Fourteen

Because God is in control, and loves us, our prayers make a difference. If God wasn't sovereign, then prayer would be a waste of time. Who wants to pray to someone who can't answer? When we pray, God never says "That's too hard for me." On the contrary, because God is all-powerful, we can pray, and it does make a difference. Prayer is the basis for every miracle.

Take time to pray about your current plans and your future plans. Ask God questions and then wait for Him to answer. Many times, we ask and then assume God doesn't care. God is always faithful to answer; we need to be faithful to wait for His answer.

Question Fifteen

This question is a launching pad for prayer requests. One of the most exciting ways to deepen faith is to pray about something and watch God answer. If you are working through this study with a group or individually, consider writing down your prayers in a journal and keeping track of the answers. Then, praise God for His sovereign nature and His love for you.

two
[GOD NEVER CHANGES]

Question One
Very few people really love change. We've heard it said, "No one likes change but a wet baby!" Isn't that true? Even the best changes in life bring elements that can create conflict. A wedding is a joyous occasion, but learning to live with someone who doesn't put the toilet paper on "right" can be frustrating. Graduating from college is fantastic, but financially supporting yourself completely can be difficult. Even the miracle of a baby is tinged with challenges when mom and dad are ready to drop from exhaustion after four months of interrupted sleep.

Acknowledging that change brings stress is important. It also helps us appreciate God's unchanging nature. When our lives are filled with changes, we can always find comfort in God's faithful character and purposes.

Question Two
This question is designed to get conversation started about personal change. Although the lesson is primarily about how God never changes, we will end the discussion with a look at how God calls us to change personally. Because we live in a sinful world, and struggle with our sin nature, God's unchanging plan for our lives will require a change on our part.

Question Three
For those blessed to be raised in a loving home, their first experience with unconditional love will be a mother or father. One characteristic of loving parents is they see the potential within their child and look past the childish, selfish behavior. This ability to look beyond the present mistakes, offers a child hope for the future. When faced with unconditional love, a child believes she is not defined by her behavior. Instead, she believes the best about herself

because of her parents' love.

When anyone offers unconditional love to another, he exhibits forgiveness. Jesus spoke about this in Matthew 18:21-22: "Then Peter came to Jesus and asked, 'Lord, how many times shall I forgive my brother when he sins against me? Up to seven times?' Jesus answered, 'I tell you, not seven times, but seventy-seven times.'" Jesus' point wasn't to give Peter numerical guidelines, but to convey there was no limit to the number of times forgiveness would be required. Thankfully, God offers this same forgiveness to us.

Question Four

In Jeremiah 31:4, God calls His people "Virgin Israel." What an amazing view God has of this rebellious group of people, who rejected Him after He had been faithful.

Years before this time, God made a promise to the Jewish nation to be their God. It was called a covenant. (Read Genesis 17:7-9) God kept His promise and expected the descendants of Abraham (the Jewish nation) to keep their promise. Unfortunately they didn't, and God had some unpleasant consequences for them as a nation. Through the prophets, God expressed His displeasure at their unfaithfulness.

In Jeremiah, God shows His true heart by wiping away their sins and choosing to see them as "virgin" or unblemished. God could have chosen to reject these wayward people. He would have been completely justified to do that. He could have left them to their own demise as they followed after false gods, and chose sinful ways. And yet God set aside their unfaithfulness and viewed them with eyes of love–eyes that saw their potential.

Question Five

It's a common practice to label ourselves by what we do. We stumble walking down the stairs and say, "I'm so clumsy." We explode in anger and say, "I'm such a jerk." Someone betrays our love, and we say, "I'm unlovable." When we betray another, we call ourselves "a loser." Those words and labels have a profound ability to affect our future. Why even try when we know the outcome will be the same?

However, when someone loves us in spite of our mistakes, or in spite of the way we have hurt him or her, we are transformed. Through unconditional love, the lies Satan tries to plant in our minds (we are worthless, unlovable, of little value) are replaced by the truth (we *are* of great worth, lovable and have immense value).

How much more transformed are we when we accept the reality of God's unchanging love for us? When we are convinced of God's love, we can shake off the chains of lies that have held us in bondage and start to become the person God wants us to be. We don't ever have to worry about losing God's love when we fall short, and that brings great freedom to explore God's calling on our lives.

Question Six

In almost every nation in the world, there can be found changes that are good and those that are bad. In the United States, our history includes the practice of legal slavery. We can thank God for men and women bold enough to stand against this horrible law and change it for the good of all.

However, we also have laws currently in place that many consider unethical. It is important to distinguish between what is legal and what is ethical. In the case of unethical laws, they should be changed. God's laws, however, never need to be changed. Because God created everything in the universe, He knows what works best. When we try and live according to any law other than God's, there will be problems.

When you were a kid, did you ever play a game with your friends where one of the kids kept changing the rules? How can anyone ever win at a game like that? The only way we can have success in life is to live according to the rules that God established.

Question Seven

God established laws, such as physical laws, which were meant to last forever. Alan Shepard, the very first American in space, was asked by a reporter just before he got into the space rocket, "What is the one thing you're depending on most in this space venture?" Shepard's answer was classic. He said, "I'm depending on the fact that God's laws never change."

Not only were God's physical laws meant to remain true forever, but so were God's moral and spiritual laws. What God laid down in the Bible was meant to last forever. God established these rules so the universe would operate in order and according to God's plans. Not only was the universe designed to work best under God's rules, but we are too.

Unfortunately, we try and "update" God's laws. Some people think it's impossible for one man and one woman to remain faithful to each other. Some believe revenge is our responsibility, lying is only a problem when someone gets hurt, and sin is only wrong if you get caught. The truth is God established some laws, principles and commands in His Word that do not change! There ARE absolutes! Some things will always be right, and some things will always be wrong!

God's rules for relationships, money and employment (to name a few) work because God designed them! We experience God's joy when we choose to honor His commands in all areas of our lives.

Question Eight

Jesus said there are two foundations upon which to build a house. (Read Matthew 7:24-27) You can build it on sand, or you can build it on a rock. Sand is forever changing. It moves with the wind and tide. Rock on the other hand, never changes. It's a solid foundation. It all comes back to what we do with the Word of God.

In a changing world, there's only one thing solid enough upon which to build our lives, and that's the Word of God. When based on the truth of God's Word, our lives, our emotions, our finances and our relationships are solid when the storms of life hit.

The unchanging quality of God's Word is a great stress reducer! We don't have to sift through what we hear Oprah say or read in *People* magazine to discern the truth. We don't have to choose between which friend or newscaster we believe. We don't have to guess at what's right or wrong. God's Word is always the best choice.

Question Nine

Have you ever worked with someone who changed his mind a lot? If so, you probably learned to write appointments with this person in pencil and held off on following orders until you were sure they were right. When you deal with someone who changes his mind a lot, you learn to distrust his word. "Watch and see" becomes the best plan of action.

With God, we don't have to second-guess His Word. What He says He'll do, He does. Not only can we trust God's Word, but His Word also has power. (Read Isaiah 55:10)

Question Ten

If you follow sewing instructions correctly, the end result will be the garment found on the cover of the pattern. This is true for any pattern we follow. Romans 12:2 cautions against following the pattern of the world: "Do not conform any longer to the pattern of this world, but be transformed by the renewing of your mind. Then you will be able to test and approve what God's will is—his good, pleasing and perfect will."

When we renew our minds with the truth of God's Word, we follow God's design. The end result will be pleasing to both God and us. Following any other pattern will result in uncertainty and a life moving farther away from God, not closer to Him.

Question Eleven

Human plans are changed by the weather, sickness, finances and our own natures. God, however, isn't affected by circumstances. God has a purpose for mankind, and instead of it being altered by events, He uses events and creation to accomplish that plan and the purposes of His heart.

Isaiah 46:10-11, confirms God's purposeful nature: "I make known the end from the beginning, from ancient times, what is still to come. I say: My purpose will stand, and I will do all that I please. From the east I summon a bird of prey; from a far-off land, a man to fulfill my purpose. What I have said, that will I bring about; what I have planned, that will I do."

Question Twelve

Our plans can change for two main reasons. The first is we don't have the perspective or foresight to know everything that's going to happen in the future. Maybe you know something now that you didn't know when you originally made your plans. With this new knowledge, your plans might change.

Another reason we change our plans is because we don't have the power to implement the changes we had intended to make. Maybe we ran out of time, money, energy or effort.

God is not like us. He is omniscient, which means He knows everything. He's also all-powerful, which means He never runs out of steam in the middle of completing a plan. With these two characteristics, God does not need to change His plans, like human beings often do.

Question Thirteen

God is for us! He wants the best for us and will do whatever it takes to accomplish that. It doesn't always look like we think it should look. But the truth is God is always working things out for our good (Romans 8:28).

Question Fourteen

If God's purpose was completely fulfilled, we would all be perfect. But we aren't. We choose to say wrong words, think wrong thoughts and do wrong deeds. We often choose a way out of alignment with God's will for us. When God's purpose isn't fulfilled, then it is our doing—not His.

Questions Fifteen and Sixteen

When we recognize that God never changes, then we must change to be like Him. The good news is that God has sent us help in the form of the Holy Spirit. We don't have to struggle and strain to change ourselves. As we renew our minds with God's Word, rest in His love and pursue His purpose, the Holy Spirit works through us to accomplish God's best for our lives.

three
[GOD'S AMAZING GRACE]

Questions One and Two

Most everybody loves to receive gifts. Many can probably remember a special gift from our childhood that stood above the rest. I (Glynnis) will never forget the Barbie car I received one Christmas. My dad was a teacher, and my mom was a homemaker, so finances were usually lean. I remember thinking it was such an extravagant gift and that I would treasure it forever. In fact, I still have it today! Gifts take on a deeper meaning when we understand the cost to the giver.

Another kind of "gift" is the gift of escaping punishment we truly deserved. It's the feeling of relief when a police car passes us by when we know we were speeding, or when a judge waives a ticket. Perhaps someone you love forgave you of a great offense. The gift of grace can bring with it a variety of emotions. There's relief, joy and even possibly guilt.

Grace on earth, receiving something we don't deserve from another person, is only a snapshot of God's grace. God's grace is a rich concept we can only begin to understand in our human minds. These first two questions are designed to get the participant thinking about the depth of grace—being given a gift we don't deserve and being forgiven sins for which we deserve punishment. Praise God for His amazing grace!

Question Three

Ephesians 2:8 tells us it is by grace we were saved. We owe our salvation entirely to God's loving-kindness to us. Our salvation is based on God's grace and mercy and not on our merit. Because God is merciful, He chooses to forgive our offenses.

Question Four

The question of how faith is developed in a human heart has been debated through the ages. Is faith something we muster up inside ourselves, or does it come from God? When this issue was being debated in the early church, there were two schools of thought which were developed by Augustine, bishop of Hippo, and Pelagius, a British monk.

Augustine was one of the foremost philosopher-theologians of early Christianity and the leading figure in the church of North Africa. On this issue of salvation, he believed that God gives us our faith. In the other court was Pelagius, who believed faith is up to us completely. Pelagius taught that man could live a sinless life, thereby earning salvation by choosing to do good, and not needing God's grace.

While today we know that Pelagius' doctrine wasn't biblical, there is a part of us that leans toward the idea that we are "responsible" for our salvation. It's somewhat disconcerting to think that even faith comes from God!

So what is our part in faith? The Zondervan NIV Study Bible makes a great point about faith: "Faith, however, is not something a person can produce; it is simply a trustful response that is itself evoked by the Holy Spirit." With that in mind, our response is to be open to whatever God wants to do in our lives.

Question Five

Salvation is based on God's promise and not on our performance. God speaks to us through His Word telling us we can never "earn" salvation, so we don't have to try. Even knowing this truth, and its resulting freedom, many people spend their entire lives trying to "earn" forgiveness and salvation, and trying to prove themselves worthy to God.

Some people believe they can have "salvation by subtraction." That means they believe if they stop doing this or that, then maybe God will forgive their sins. They have a list of "don'ts" that guide their lives. You probably know some of these don'ts: don't smoke, cuss or chew, or go with girls who do!

Then there's "salvation by service." That means if you just do nice things for others, you'll get to heaven. So some people exhaust themselves at church, or serving in worthwhile organizations in order to please God enough that He'll have to grant them salvation.

One other type of salvation people try to grasp is "salvation through comparison." They might say something like, "I'm better than so-and-so, and they're a Christian!" The fact is, you may be a better person than someone else, but God doesn't judge us in comparison to each other. That's the meaning of salvation by grace. The only "person" we are compared to is God Himself, and we can never measure up! We need God's grace.

Question Six

God demonstrated His amazing grace by sending His Son, Jesus Christ, to die for our sins. It is through our faith in Jesus that we are washed clean of guilt. Romans 3:22-23 tells us, "This righteousness from God comes through faith in Jesus Christ to all who believe. There is no difference, for all have sinned and fall short of the glory of God ..."

Not one of us is perfect! We all make mistakes, and we all have feelings of guilt because of that. But the good news is Jesus Christ has already paid for our sins. We have to accept His free gift. So there's no reason for us to carry around unnecessary guilt.

This is one of the most basic truths in the Christian life! God's saving grace removes our guilt! If we could save ourselves, then Jesus going to the cross was a waste. There would've been no reason for Jesus to die if we could save ourselves. We simply can't!

Question Seven

As Christians, we gain strength from reading God's Word, hearing it taught, and from having fellowship with other Christians. In this passage in Hebrews, we are urged to remember that our spiritual strength comes from God's grace.

It's human nature to want to do something to gain strength. Athletes train to gain physical strength. Scholars study to gain mental strength. Christians try to gain spiritual strength by obeying rules and following the teachings of others. Yet the writer of Hebrews warns against such empty pursuits.

Through God's grace, and the faith He provides, we have all we need to have our hearts strengthened. Faith that God is in control, that He is working things out for our good, and that He loves us, provides strength to our inner selves that no amount of outward actions can create.

Question Eight

One of the biggest problems in Christianity is that people start their Christian faith by beginning a relationship with Jesus Christ and then somewhere along the line they fall back into a religious syndrome of following rules and regulations. Oftentimes, new Christians are just happy to be in love with God, which gives them sincere strength of purpose. That's enough until they make the dangerous mistake of watching certain other Christians–how they dress, act, or the spiritual phrases they use. When we watch other people, we can create our own list of religious rules on how to act. Then, we start basing our decisions on what other people will think of us.

Another false sense of security comes when we follow man-made rules in churches, either written or unwritten. We might hope to gain confidence if we buy a certain Bible, wear a certain suit, or bow our heads in a specific way. Then, just maybe, God won't look at what's going on inside our hearts. Any time we shift our source of strength outside of God's grace, we miss what God wants to do in our hearts, which is to completely revamp them!

Question Nine

Understanding God's grace helps keep us humble and seeking God's truth. When we truly understand that everything we have comes from God, even our faith, we realize our complete dependence upon God. Anytime we are faced with teaching that seems contradictory to the Bible, we know not to trust what "sounds" good, but to seek the truth directly from God's Word.

Question Ten

Before Paul became a Christian, his name was Saul, and he was a leading persecutor of Christians. In Acts chapter nine, we read about Saul's miraculous conversion to Christianity. From that time, Paul received many revelations from God, and this passage shows his awareness of the potential for those visions to bring him spiritual harm. No one is certain about the exact nature of the thorn Paul experienced. But we know the Lord decided to not remove the thorn, thereby teaching Paul, and us, a profound lesson.

Paul, himself, tells us the benefit of the thorn in the very first part of the Second Corinthians passage. The benefit is "To keep me from becoming conceited because of these surpassingly great revelations." Earlier, in verse one, Paul refers to the "visions and revelations from the Lord." Paul identifies the spiritual benefit to be one of humility. In spite of the great faith Paul experienced, and the miraculous visions, God kept Paul without conceit, by allowing an irritant to remain in his life.

Question Eleven

Paul pleaded with God to remove the thorn, but the answer was "no." The truth is, we would never learn anything if all our problems were instantly removed as soon as we prayed about them. We can almost always learn more through pain than we do through pleasure! So sometimes God chooses to leave the pain in our lives.

Romans 8:28 tells us, "And we know that in all things God works for the good of those who love him, who have been called according to his purpose." Sometimes the "good" in our problems comes from learning to rely more on God. When we do that, we learn about His character and His love. Sometimes the "good" is that our character is developed and strengthened. God looks at our good differently than we do.

Question Twelve

Human weakness provides the perfect palette for God's glory and power to be revealed. Throughout the Bible we read stories of God choosing to work through weak and imperfect people. Moses was a murderer in hiding when God spoke to him through a burning bush. David was an insignificant shepherd boy when God chose him to be king. Rahab was a prostitute when God called her to bravely hide two Israelite spies. The list goes on.

God chooses to work through people who allow Him to shine and get the glory! When someone is convinced of his or her own strength, his pride hinders the work God can do. Our weakness allows God's will to be done, instead of ours.

Question Thirteen

When we try to handle a hurt or a problem on our own, we can get bitter. Hebrews 12:15 warns, "See to it that no one comes short of the grace of God; that no root of bitterness springing up causes trouble, and by it many defiled" (NASB). By attempting to handle a problem without God's grace, we can become resentful.

It's so easy to become cynical, critical and bitter. Sometimes people even raise their fist toward God and say, "Why me?" They begin having a pity party for themselves, saying things like "Poor me, look at this problem in my life." When that happens, it's easy to stop relying on the grace of God.

As a pastor, I (Brian) meet hurting people all the time. It amazes me that you can take two people, put them in the exact same situation and one will be devastated and end up resentful, while the other ends up having a sweet spirit and growing spiritually because of it. Why is that? Because the people who end up having a sweet spirit are those who rely on the sustaining grace of God and not on themselves.

Questions Fourteen and Fifteen

The key to receiving God's grace in our lives is to admit that we need it. That's really all it takes–just admit that we need God. Pride prevents God's grace. As long as I'm self-dependent, as long as I have the attitude "I can handle it!" or "I don't need anyone to help me," then I'll never receive God's grace in my life. In fact, according to the passage in James, God will oppose me when I have that kind of prideful attitude.

If we humble ourselves before God, and tell Him how much we need Him and His grace in our lives, then God starts to release grace to us. We can choose the path of humility by making everyday choices to combat our pride. We can be honest about own weaknesses to start with, confessing our weaknesses to God and others. When we are honest with ourselves and with others, pride loses its grip on our hearts.

four

[GOD CAN BE TRUSTED]

Questions One and Two

Keeping a promise tells a lot about a person's integrity. Some promises are easy to keep—like telling someone you'll take them out to dinner. Other promises are more difficult to keep—like promising to pay back a loan or remain faithful in marriage.

We've each been the recipient of a broken promise, and depending on the type of promise, our reactions can range from mildly annoyed to totally devastated.

On the other hand, faithfulness is a valued commodity in our world. A friend who sticks by us during a major illness is a treasure. A company that refuses to lay off employees during difficult times ranks high in our esteem. A leader whose life is consistent with her spoken values is highly respected. We want to trust people, and when they prove themselves trustworthy, we love them even more.

Question Three

Everyone needs guidance in his or her life from time to time. You may even have a decision weighing on you right now, and are wondering what to do. We face decisions, both small and large, every day. What to eat for breakfast, what to wear, which road to take to work or school. Our decisions can be based on how we feel that day, the weather and if the morning news announces a traffic accident on our normal commute.

Unfortunately, many people look to sources other than God's Word for the big decisions in life. We turn to friends, family, even our checkbooks to help give us guidance. Some people even turn to sources such as horoscopes, tea leaves, crystals and the psychic hotline! Bookstores abound with "self-help" books filled with "guidance" for whatever problem you are facing.

The problem with all those sources is they are undependable. It's not that you can't depend on your friends to give you good advice; Christians should seek the counsel of godly, mature Christians. Proverbs 24:6 says, "For by wise guidance you will wage war, and in abundance of counselors there is victory" (NASB). However, even the wisest person on earth is a weak replacement for God's wisdom.

As we read the Bible and study God's principles, we will become more and more acquainted with the ways of God. Then, when faced with a decision, we can trust that God has already given us trustworthy guidance through His Word.

Question Four

Proverbs 3:5-6 cautions us to not "lean on your own understanding." That's because our understanding of any situation is shaded by our past experience, our hurts, our fears and our hopes.

Unfortunately, we can't always trust our understanding because our hearts are deceitful. Jeremiah 17:9 says, "The human heart is the most deceitful of all things, and desperately wicked. Who really knows how bad it is?" (NLT)

This verse comes after some very harsh words from the Lord found in verse 5, "This is what the LORD says: 'Cursed are those who put their trust in mere humans, who rely on human strength and turn their hearts away from the LORD. They are like stunted shrubs in the desert, with no hope for the future. They will live in the barren wilderness, in an uninhabited salty land.'"

God calls us to trust in Him, and His ways, instead of what "seems right" to us. This means we have to know God's ways, and we find that in Scripture. We should always seek to know more of the Bible, and participating in this study is one way to help you learn more about God's ways.

Question Five

Acknowledging the Lord in all our ways, starts with an understanding that God cares about every part of our lives. The Bible is filled with commandments and counsel on everything from work to relationships. It also gives us guidance on how to resolve conflict, whether or not to borrow money, how to respect authority, what to look at, what to say, what not to say and more. God wants us to know His ways, and has revealed them in Scripture.

It's easy, but dangerous, to compartmentalize our lives. This passage in Proverbs makes it clear that God wants us to acknowledge Him in all areas of our lives. Here are some ways we can acknowledge God every day:

How we use our time at work
How we speak to our children
Serving in an area of ministry at church
If we open our home to friends and family
Whether we tithe or not
If we show courtesy on the roads or in a store

Question Six

This question will require you to know some Scripture. If there's a member of the group who is a new Christian, please initiate help and encouragement. It's possible a new Christian won't have enough biblical knowledge to know if he or she has made any decisions based on the Bible.

A great place to start is by reviewing the Ten Commandments. These commandments still apply to us today and can be found in Exodus 20. For those with little biblical knowledge, they can learn some very basic guidelines for life.

Question Seven

If we are honest with ourselves, we will admit that we have sought our own forms of revenge at times. Little kids seem to do this naturally, which is evidence that we aren't born choosing to do good. If Susan didn't invite Megan to her birthday party, then Megan will leave Susan off her guest list. If Mark got left out of a pick-up football game by his friend Jeff, you can be sure Mark will "forget" to invite Jeff the next time there's a neighborhood game.

Adults aren't too different from kids at times. If someone snubs us, we determine to avoid him. If someone gossips about us, then it's easier to speak badly about her. This question will require some honesty. However, since God said not to seek revenge, we should address the ways in which we do.

Question Eight

God is very much aware of what people do to you! He knows when you've been put down, hurt, stabbed in the back, maligned, slandered and so on. In fact, He even knows things that you don't. God gives you two options when people hurt you: defend yourself or let God defend you! Who do you think will do a better job of it? Who has better resources to defend you? God, of course!

Not only is God a better defender, but because of God's perfect nature, He can mete out justice fairly. Even Jesus, who could have called hundreds of angels to protect Him, left His defense in the hands of God. In 1 Peter 2:23 we read, "He did not retaliate when he was insulted. When he suffered, he did not threaten to get even. He left his case in the hands of God, who always judges fairly" (NLT).

One other reason God wants to be our defender is that when we seek revenge, we can easily make sinful decisions. Then we will be as guilty as the one who has wronged us! When we let God settle the score, and we forgive the offender, we have a clean heart.

Question Nine

One very effective way to forgive and love our enemies is to remember the great love God showed us while we were still offending Him. Romans 5:6-8 speaks powerful words about how God forgave us. When we remember that God forgave us, it helps us keep the right perspective. It also helps to remember that Jesus Himself suffered. When we are hurt, especially for Jesus' sake, we are sharing in His suffering. (Read 1 Peter 4:12-14.)

Question Ten

Luke 6:38 makes it clear that the condition for receiving in abundance is giving.

There are two principles that could be at work here. One is the principle of sowing and reaping. Second Corinthians 9:6-7 says, "Remember this: Whoever sows sparingly will also reap sparingly, and whoever sows generously will also reap generously. Each man should give what he has decided in his heart to give, not reluctantly or under compulsion, for God loves a cheerful giver" (NIV).

Although this speaks of giving financially, the principle of reaping and sowing is a biblically sound one.

The other reason God may require that we make the first move is to prove our obedience. Anyone can say he is a follower of God. The truth is in his actions. James 2:17-18 says, "Even so faith, if it has no works, is dead, being by itself. But someone may well say, 'You have faith and I have works; show me your faith without the works, and I will show you my faith by my works'" (NASB). When we obey, we show where our hearts really lie.

Question Eleven

This question offers participants a wonderful opportunity to praise God for His faithfulness. As you share stories of God's goodness, take time to thank God for doing what He promised.

Question Twelve

In this particular verse, we are called to "confess." We need to confess, or "agree with God" about our sins. The promise is that God will forgive. This verse doesn't say anything about "working" for our forgiveness. We don't have to do some kind of "penance" to earn God's forgiveness – even though it's in our nature to try. We tell God things like: "If you'll just forgive me one more time, I'll never do it again!" Or we try and bribe God, "If you'll just forgive me, then I'll give 20% of my income to You!" We can even try to beg God to forgive us. "Please, please, please forgive me!!!"

We don't need to bargain with God, bribe God or beg God to get Him to forgive our sins. We just need to confess our sins and God says "I will forgive you!" Why? Because He is faithful. He said He would ... so He will!

Question Thirteen

Satan blinds us to the truth about our own sin. Starting in the Garden of Eden, Satan tried to convince Eve that God didn't really mean what He said. Satan still tries those deceptive tricks on us – and they oftentimes work! Satan wants us to believe that what God has called "sin," isn't really sin.

In Acts 26, Paul is telling about his encounter with Jesus on the road to Damascus. Jesus gave Paul the commandment to be a witness to what He had seen. Jesus also had this requirement of Paul: "I am sending you to them to open their eyes and turn them from darkness to light, and from the power of Satan to God, so that they may receive forgiveness of sins and a place among those who are sanctified by faith in me" (verse 17-18 NIV).

We are called to turn from darkness to light, which involves having our eyes open to our sin and confessing that sin.

Question Fourteen

Each of us responds differently to God's forgiveness. When we truly understand our need for a savior, we should live our lives with a deep, abiding gratitude. It's when we get complacent about our sin that we begin to take God's faithfulness for granted.

Questions Fifteen and Sixteen

This study has addressed only four of the ways that God can be trusted. We've studied how God gives us guidance, how God defends us, how God rewards our generosity and how God forgives our sins. We can also trust God to remember our service, to comfort us, and to give us wisdom. If you are in a group study, brainstorm other ways that God is faithful.

five
[GOD IS ALWAYS NEAR]

Questions One and Two

For many of us, friendships are whipped cream on the ice cream sundae of life. They are an added bonus, but not essential. However, God thinks otherwise. In Ecclesiastes 4:8-10 we have the following words of advice: "Two are better than one, because they have a good return for their work: If one falls down, his friend can help him up. But pity the man who falls and has no one to help him up!"

As wonderful as friendships are, even the best friend disappoints us at times. That's why it's important for every Christian to know God and develop a relationship with Him. God is the only one who will never leave us or forsake us. As we think about the benefits of our human friends, it's important to consider how we can experience those same benefits with God. The first two questions in this study should open the door to consider how knowing God enriches our lives even more than knowing a friend.

Question Three

We live in a world with more than six billion inhabitants, and yet people everywhere are lonely. There are many reasons for loneliness, and many types of loneliness. There's the loneliness of the death of a spouse, the loss of a friend, a business trip, a new school, moving, growing old, a loveless marriage, or just feeling like no one understands you.

Our technology-rich society inhibits social interaction like never before. E-mail replaces phone calls, which replace personal visits. Blogs replace letters. The Internet opens our world to human contact and closes it at the same time. Employees tele-commute, business associates tele-conference and our best friend is the television! This is all very telling about why we are lonely! We think we hardly need each other.

Question Four

In Hebrews 13:5 God is quoted as saying, "Never will I leave you; never will I forsake you." The origin of these exact words isn't clear. However, there are a number of similar statements in the Old Testament. Apparently, even the godliest men of faith needed to be reminded of God's presence.

God told Jacob, "I am with you and will watch over you wherever you go, and I will bring you back to this land. I will not leave you until I have done what I have promised you" (Genesis 28:15).

Moses told Joshua that God was always present based on his personal experience. "Be strong and courageous. Do not be afraid or terrified because of them, for the LORD your God goes with you; he will never leave you nor forsake you" (Deuteronomy 31:6).

Apparently Joshua needed to hear it again. After the death of Moses, God told Joshua directly, "As I was with Moses, so I will be with you; I will never leave you nor forsake you" (Joshua 1:5).

God reminded His chosen people of His presence, just as He reminds us of His presence. Although we can't see God, we can be assured that He is near.

Question Five

The thirteenth chapter of Hebrews is a wrap-up of the entire letter and includes a series of exhortations. The readers of this letter were encouraged about some practical points of living the Christian life. The warning in Hebrews 13: 5 is to "Keep your lives free from the love of money and be content with what you have."

Question Six

The love of money and lack of contentment are just two reasons people experience loneliness. Both of these conditions reflect unhappiness with what we have. We were each created with a need for God planted in our hearts. When we search for satisfaction outside of a relationship with God, we end up empty and lonely.

It's not just the desire for money and possessions that leads to emptiness. We covet human interaction that we think will erase our loneliness. A single person thinks being married is the answer to loneliness and misses the rich opportunity to invest time in knowing God now. A businessman thinks the happy-hour gang will fill his longing to find someone who cares. A student wishes she were among the "in-crowd" so she could have a friend. When we are constantly on the lookout for relationships to fill our needs, we can miss what we already have—and that's the presence of God every minute of the day.

Question Seven

The first truth we learn from this passage is that temptation is common to all of us. This is no surprise since we know the truth about ourselves. However, it is somewhat reassuring to know we are not alone in our struggles. People often think they have a unique problem or temptation, but that's not true! We all have the same, or at least similar, problems.

Even Jesus was tempted. Hebrews 2:18 says, "Because he himself suffered when he was tempted, he is able to help those who are being tempted." Despite being tempted, Jesus never sinned. Hebrews 4:15 confirms this: "For we do not have a high priest who is unable to sympathize with our weaknesses, but we have one who has been tempted in every way, just as we are—yet was without sin."

The Bible records one situation in which Jesus was tempted. In Matthew chapter four, Satan tempted Jesus in the desert using three different common temptations. Before starting the temptation, the devil first made sure Jesus was weakened after fasting for 40 days. Then Satan tried to tempt Jesus in three areas: 1) Jesus' physical satisfaction, 2) Jesus' security, and 3) His desire for power.

These are three common areas of temptation for us too. We are tempted to sin in areas of physical satisfaction. This can involve anything that meets a physical need or a want. We also are tempted with false security, such as money or a job. Finally, we are lured to sin with the promise of power. Your group might take some time to identify specific examples in these three areas.

Question Eight

Knowing God is faithful, as mentioned in the 1 Corinthians passage, encourages us to be faithful in return. When someone loves us with unconditional love and faithfulness, the thought of disappointing him or her is often a deterrent to succumbing to temptation.

Jesus models another way of escape and that's the truth of Scripture. For every temptation that Satan proposed in Matthew 4, Jesus was ready with a Scripture. After the third temptation, Jesus ordered Satan to leave Him and he left.

A great way to deal with our personal temptations is to memorize Scripture that speaks truth into our minds and hearts. Use a Bible concordance and research pertinent Bible verses.

Question Nine

Knowing God is right next to us at all times is a strong motivation to flee from temptation. Who wants to sin right in front of God? We need to be clear on this truth—God sees every sin we commit. Proverbs 15:3 says, "The eyes of the Lord are in every place, watching the evil and the good" (NASB).

It's easier to control our behavior when we know others are watching us. You wouldn't go to an all-you-can-eat restaurant and pull up a chair to the buffet line. There are all kinds of behaviors we restrain in public. That's because when people watch us, we are motivated to polite behavior. When we are aware of God's presence, it can help us maintain more control over our temptations.

Question Ten

Trouble is a part of life on earth. We are either coming out of a time of trouble, in trouble or about to go through trouble! Isaiah 43:2 confirms this fact. This passage doesn't say God will be with us "if" we pass through water, it says "when" we pass through water, the rivers and the fire. This Scripture is laden with memories and reminders of God's faithfulness to the Israelites. They told and re-told the story of God leading the Israelites out of slavery in Egypt. They knew God dried up the Red Sea and the Jordan River so their ancestors could escape Pharaoh's army.

This passage in Isaiah 43:2 affirms God's nearness and protection over His people. God promises to be with us and protect us from being overwhelmed and destroyed by our troubles. It doesn't say our troubles will be eliminated, but with God's presence, we will overcome our troubles. In our trouble, God is not a passive bystander, but a source of help. This brings us great confidence.

Question Eleven

King David knew the confidence God's presence can provide. In Psalm 16:8-9 he wrote, "I know the Lord is always with me. I will not be shaken, for he is right beside me. No wonder my heart is filled with joy and my mouth shouts his praises! My body rests in safety." God's presence in our lives is a stress reliever. We can have confidence that with God's help, we can handle anything that comes our way. That confidence doesn't come from psychology. It only comes from knowing God is with me and working for me.

Question Twelve

This question allows the participants to honestly admit some of their personal discouragements. Depending on the trust level in your group, some people may have a difficult time sharing this information with others. Discouragement is often a result of something personally embarrassing. We might fail at something, get passed by for a promotion, or rejected by someone we love. When these things happen, a common response is discouragement, then giving up. On top of that, we don't share the discouragement because it's embarrassing.

We say things like, "I'm not going to put any more effort into this business! I'm not going to put any more effort into this marriage! I'm not going to try that again!" Self-esteem is crushed, dreams are shattered and hope is gone. Life is filled with discouragement because that's Satan's plan for us. Thankfully, God has another plan for us.

Question Thirteen

Whereas Satan wants to destroy us, God wants to bring us life. God is always for us; never against us. This is a truth that we can easily forget in times of discouragement, but brings great comfort. Some other truths about God that bring us comfort include:
- God loves us unconditionally.
- God has a plan for our lives.

- God never gives up on us.
- God is always faithful.

This question can provide an opportunity for praising God. Perhaps your group can make a list of everyone's answers and incorporate them into your time of worship and prayer. Our God is great! We need to remember all His attributes and recount them to each other and praise God for who He is.

Question Fourteen

In order to fully experience the presence of God, we need to surrender all areas of our lives to Jesus Christ. This means acknowledging Jesus as Lord not only on Sunday, but on every day of the week. It means submitting to God's way in our time, finances, relationships, jobs and recreation. There's no area of our lives that should be off-limits to the Lordship of Jesus Christ.

When we say, "God—You can have Sundays, but I get to do what I want the other six days of the week!" we effectively close ourselves to His presence. It's not that God's not there. We don't experience His presence when we aren't surrendered. Being fully surrendered often involves a close examination of our hearts. It might be helpful to pray the psalmist's prayer before answering this question. (Read Psalm 139:23-24)

Question Fifteen

A major reason people never feel the presence of God is because they are just too busy and distracted. Something is always on–the television, radio, CD player or I-Pod. Even satellite radio assures you are never too far away to hear something! Psalm 46:10a says, "Be still and know that I am God." The problem is unless we are just about to fall asleep, many of us are seldom still and quiet. Several times a day, we need to tune into God's presence and "drop out" of the environment around us. We can just take a few minutes wherever we are and say, "God, I realize you're present with me right now! I just want to take a few minutes to recognize Your presence and thank You for all the great things that You do for me each and every day."

six

[GOD LOVES YOU]

Question One

Love, as portrayed on television and movies, leaves much to be desired. If we learned about love from watching on-screen relationships, we would understand it to be based on a shallow foundation of attraction and convenience. We would believe that love lasted as long as the needs of both individuals were being met. If a need was unfulfilled, then it would be time to end the relationship and move on to someone who could meet the need. Love in the movies is mostly about receiving and less about giving. It's about comfort and not sacrifice. Basically, if we learned about love from the movies, we would think it went from the euphoria of early love to a break-up with very little time in between.

Of course, that observation is a generalization. It is possible to find examples of selfless and faithful love in the movies. But the persevering love that suffers through the monotony of life doesn't always make for good ticket sales! We want drama and flair, and a promise that the honeymoon will last forever!

Question Two

Because God made us unique, every person's answer to this question will be different. Author Gary Chapman wrote a groundbreaking book called *The Five Love Languages.* In it, he identified five ways to communicate and understand emotional love: words of affirmation, quality time, receiving gifts, acts of service and personal touch. Not only does it help to learn how we understand love, but we should take the time to learn the "love language" of those we care about.

When we think about our love languages and God, it's amazing to realize that He has the ability to communicate His love in all of these languages if we are attentive to His voice and ways. While we may not feel His physical touch, He most certainly sends people our way to fulfill that need. God knows our need for love and is pleased to shower His love upon us. If you are doing this study in a group, take notes on what speaks love to those in your group. This can be a way you can minister to them in the future.

Question Three

God is not a God of words alone, but of action. Every promise He has made, He has fulfilled. Second Corinthians 1:20 tells us, "For no matter how many promises God has made, they are 'Yes' in Christ. And so through him the 'Amen' is spoken by us to the glory of God."

Jesus is the proof of God's great love to us! God demonstrated this love by offering His beloved Son to a world that scorned and rejected Him, so that through Jesus, some might come to experience eternal life with God. (Romans 5:8) Understanding this love is hard for anyone, but for a parent, it's almost unfathomable. To offer your child's life for the life of another, especially someone who didn't appreciate the sacrifice, seems impossible. And yet God loves us that much!

Question Four

The Bible is filled with God's promises to those who believe in His Son. Jesus taught that God is a loving Father who willingly gives good things to His children when they ask. (Matthew 7:9-11)

When we read Scripture with an eye for evidence of God's love, we find that He generously gives to everyone. In Philippians 4:19 we are told God will supply all our needs. In 2 Corinthians 12:9 Paul tells us that God's grace is sufficient for us. In First Corinthians 10:13 we learn that God will "not allow you to be tempted beyond what you are able, but with the temptation will provide the way of escape also, so that you will be able to endure it." One additional proof of God's love is the peace He gives in the midst of trouble. (Philippians 4:7)

Although God loves us with an extravagant love, be aware that His promises are often conditional. Look for the word "if" in Scripture. This doesn't diminish God's love; it just shows that He's concerned with our character as much as meeting our needs.

Question Five

Some people avoid God because they believe He will make them give up their fun. They believe that being spiritual is equivalent with being miserable. The problem is that television and movies give us a particular image of "fun." Advertisers sell the lie that if you buy their product, you'll be happy and have fun! Unfortunately, that type of "fun" quickly wears off. So you end up buying something else, and that "fun" wears off too.

Others reject God's love because they're afraid people will think they are a fanatic. Oftentimes, well-meaning, but misguided Christians cause others to avoid God because of their fanaticism. Their over-the-top brand of religion seems hard to grasp for someone just getting to know God. The good news is that Jesus said that He came that we might have life, not religion. When we look at our objections for not accepting God's love, they are often based on fear. The only way to fight fear is with fact. (1 Timothy 6:17)

Question Six

Although God loves us unconditionally, He does not force Himself or His commands upon us. Additionally, God wants what is best for us, which means He doesn't let us get away with any sort of sin that we want to commit. As a wise parent, He sets consequences for our choices. If we choose to obey, we are rewarded (Luke 6:35, 1 Corinthians 3:8). If we choose to disobey, then we suffer the results of that choice.

Question Seven

Human love, without God's love as its foundation, wears out easily due to our limited attention span, our fickle natures or changing fads. A teenage crush is a good example of a short-term love. Marriages that are solely based on physical attraction easily wear out when the beauty is gone. We might claim to feel "love" for a favorite food, a car or a certain outfit. That "love" is definitely superficial!

Question Eight

As a sign of her undying love and faithfulness, a certain celebrity permanently tattooed the name of her beloved on her arm. This act of affection was "permanent" until she and the love of her life broke up. Then the tattoo was removed, and another's name tattooed in its place. So much for everlasting love!

Human love wears out! That's why there are so many divorces today. The reasons why human love wears out are varied and often complicated. One reason human love wears out is that people start loving with the expectation that it will cease. They fully expect that love will end. So when the other person fails to meet their expectations, they are ready to stop "loving." In other words, it is conditional. We put conditions on those we promise to love. We can even put conditions on our children. This is a stark contrast to God's love.

Though others may stop loving us, God will not. To make sure we know He's serious, God made two eternally permanent marks of His faithful love. First, in Isaiah 49:16 God tells us, "See, I have engraved you on the palms of my hands."

Then, God made His second mark of faithfulness with the blood of Jesus. Ephesians 2:13, "But now in Christ Jesus you who once were far away have been brought near through the blood of Christ." The cross is our reminder of that love.

Question Nine

Although 1 Corinthians 13:4-8a offers an outline for the love we should show to each other, it also offers a list of words to describe God's love:

"Love is patient, love is kind. It does not envy, it does not boast, it is not proud. It is not rude, it is not self-seeking, it is not easily angered, it keeps no record of wrongs. Love does not delight in evil but rejoices with the truth. It always protects, always trusts, always hopes, always perseveres. Love never fails."

Question Ten

In reading chapter 8 of Romans, one can almost hear Paul's awe of God's majesty and all-encompassing love. Paul is convinced that nothing on earth nor in the supernatural realm can separate us from God's love that is found in Jesus. Death cannot separate us because as believers in Jesus, we will be with God forever. Life and all its attractions and trials (including our own wrong choices) will not stop God from loving us. Even though Satan and his demons are out for our harm, even they can't interfere with God's love. If there is anything Paul hasn't thought of, he wraps up these passages with a broad sweep encompassing all creation.

Question Eleven

God will never leave us. In Hebrews 13:5 God says, "Never will I leave you; never will I forsake you." No matter where we go, God is there. However, some people don't experience God's love despite His ever-present nearness. When that happens, they will experience loneliness no matter how many people they are with. The converse is true; when we know God's love, we're never alone.

Question Twelve

Even the newest Christian can see God's loving kindness in some area of his or her life. For a Christian, nothing is coincidence or luck. Every good thing we experience is from the hand of our loving Heavenly Father.

Question Thirteen

When God doesn't answer our prayers exactly as we prayed them, it's human nature to think it's a sign of His lack of love or care. We have been conditioned to think that "true love" is demonstrated by the giving of something bright and shiny, and the more carats the better! It's an age-old joke that if a husband buys his wife something "useful" (aka a vacuum cleaner) he better be prepared to sleep on the couch. However, God demonstrates His love in just that way–giving us what we need, not what we want. We may think we "need" a new car, but God knows what we truly need.

To overcome any disappointment, read through the Scriptures to better understand the character of God and what He thinks is really important.

Question Fourteen

Even the most mature Christian can have moments of doubt. Doubt is not always a sign of our lack of faith, but of our humanness. It's important to be honest about those times and share them with someone you can trust. Together you can pray for God to reveal His love and to help you overcome your doubt. Ask God to help you see signs of His love, and then watch with expectancy.

Question Fifteen

Regardless of your situation, regardless of your background, God has arranged for you to participate in this study so that He can tell you of His love. You matter so much to God that He sent Jesus to die on the cross for you. That is the ultimate demonstration of love. When faced with God's amazing love for us, how can we help but love Him back and surrender the control of our lives to Him? Even if you have been far from God, He still says, "With deep love I will take you back" (Isaiah 54:7b, Good News).

If you enjoyed this study, be sure to check out other studies in the Kingdom Living series at ampelonpublishing.com

such as ...
"Worship: Nearing the Heart of God"
... or ...
"Six Habits of Highly Effective Christians"